Sayyid

A Selective Annotated Bibliography of Dissertations and Theses

A. Jefferson Kilpatrick

Copyright © 2015 A. Jefferson Kilpatrick

All rights reserved.

No part of this book may be used or reproduced in any manner whatsoever without the written permission of the author.

Kilpatrick, A. Jefferson

Sayyid Qutb: A selective annotated bibliography of dissertations and theses/A. Jefferson Kilpatrick

p. cm.

1. Sayyid Qutb (1906-1966) -- Criticism and Interpretation. 2. Islam and Politics -- Egypt. I. Title.

BP 130.4
297.1977

ISBN-10   1515105407

ISBN-13   978-1515105404

Table of Contents

1.) **Al-Sulaim, F. A.** 1
The Arab Nahdha projects and the Arab intellectuals' perspectives of modernity and social change in the Arab world.

2.) **Bakhtiari, B.** 4
Religion and politics: The Middle East and Latin America.

3.) **Barnes, L. A.** 7
Sayyid Qutb: "Pious hero of Islam"* or terrorist theoretician?

4.) **Bouzid, A. T.** 9
Man, society, and knowledge in the Islamist discourse of Sayyid Qutb.

5.) **Bozek, J. D.** 13
Sayyid Qutb: An historical and contextual analysis of jihadist theory.

6.) **Calvert, J. C. M.** 15
Discourse, community and power: Sayyid Qutb and the Islamic movement in Egypt.

7.) **Edens, M. H.** 17
An evangelical Christian response to concepts of humanity found in selected Islamic writings.

8.) **Elfenbein, C. H. I.** 20
Differentiating Islam: Colonialism, Sayyid Qutb, and religious transformation in modern Egypt.

9.) **Elgindy, A.** 23
Translation and the construction of the religious other: A sociological approach to English translations of Islamic political discourse.

10.) **Euben, R. L.** 25
Islamic fundamentalism and the limits of modern rationalism.

11.)   **Frisk, W. H.** **28**
The Vanguards of Islamism: Origins, Histories, and Ideologies of the Society of Muslim Brothers in Egypt.

12.)   **Gelineau, J.** **31**
Threat and Political Opportunity and the Development of the Egyptian Muslim Brotherhood.

13.)   **Hassan, F. M.** **33**
Ending oppression and establishing justice: Examples from Islamic history of select Muslims and Islamist groups justifying the use of armed force.

14.)   **Hawwari, A. A. S.** **36**
Challenging the incompatibility paradigm: A democratic audit of Jordan, 1990-2010.

15.)   **Horowitz, J.** **39**
An examination of how American business must eliminate perceived bias towards Muslims and Arab Americans.

16.) **Hosein, J.** 43
A Cross Examination of Sayyid Qutb and Muhammad Ibn Abd Al-Wahhab.

17.) **Isaacson, T. J.** 45
Miracles and militancy: The evental origins of religious revolution.

18.) **Jackson, R. A.** 47
A Nietzschean approach to key Islamic paradigms.

19.) **Kozak, A. M.** 50
Reconceptualization of democracy from an Islamic subaltern.

20.) **LaRossa, C.** 55
The development of Islamic political thought in relation to the West during the mid-twentieth century.

21.) **Leary, J. D.** 57
Beyond Al-Qa'ida: The theology, transformation and global growth of Salafi radicalism since 1979.

22.) **Moussalli, A. S.** 59
Contemporary Islamic political thought: Sayyid Qutb.

23.) **Mubarak, H.** 63
Intersections: Modernity, gender, and Qur'anic exegesis.

24.) **Munro, M. A.** 66
Religion and revolution in Egypt.

25.) **Musallam, A. A.** 68
The formative stages of Sayyid Qutb's intellectual career and his emergence as an Islamic Da'iyah, 1906-1952.

26.) **Mussad, H. W.** 71
Muslim debate on the adoption of the Shari'a and its implications for the Church.

27.) **Mussad, H. W.** 73
Theology of the Muslim fundamentalist Sayyid Qutb.

28.) **Oh, I. Y. I.** 75
Human rights in contemporary Islamic thought: Toward a cross-cultural discourse ethic.

29.) **Rahman, S.** 78
The concept of takfir (accusing of disbelief) among some contemporary Islamic movements with special reference to Egypt.

30.) **Roald, A. S.** 81
Tarbiya: Education and politics in Islamic movements in Jordan and Malaysia.

31.) **Salihu, F.** 84
Assemblages of radicalism: The online recruitment practices of Islamist terrorists.

32.) **Sayilgan, M. S.** 86
Constructing an Islamic ethics of non-violence: The case of Bediuzzaman Said Nursi.

33.) **Shah Bin Jani, M.** 88
Sayyid Qutb's view of jihad; an analytical study of his major works.

34.) **Shaikh, E. M.** 90
War and peace: Towards an understanding of the theology of jihad.

35.) **Steiner, J. G.** 92
The psychology of terrorism: A case study of Osama bin Laden.

36.) **Suarez-Murias, A.** 95
"Jihad is the way and death for the sake of Allah is our highest aspiration": A narrative analysis of Sayyid Qutb's "Milestones."

37.) **Syahnan, M.** 97
A study of Sayyid Qutb's Qur'an exegesis in earlier and later editions of his "Fi Zilal al-Qur'an" with specific reference to selected themes.

38.) **Winkel, E. A.** **99**
The ontological status of politics in Islam and the epistemology of Islamic revival.

39.) **Yunus, M. R.** **101**
Modern approaches to the study of i'jaz al-Qur'an.

Locating Dissertations and Theses 103

Sayyid Qutb

A Selective Annotated Bibliography of Dissertations and Theses

1.) **Al-Sulaim, F. A.**
The Arab Nahdha projects and the Arab intellectuals' perspectives of modernity and social change in the Arab world.
Ph.D. dissertation, American University. 2004.

Since the introduction of modernity to the Arab World in 1798, the Arab World has experienced three attempts of modernization called (Arab Nahdha projects). These projects served as the theoretical and practical agenda for social change, designed for achieving liberty, progress and prosperity. The first two projects (1815-1837, and 1952-1970) failed, and the Arab World is currently going through the third attempt. The failure of the Nahdha projects, and the persistence of backwardness of the Arab World have resulted in rich and diverse intellectual writings about modernity and the desired social change in the Arab World. This qualitative study analyzes the Arab intellectuals' perspectives regarding modernity and social change in the Arab World. A classification of the main trends and currents of the Arab Intellectuals' thoughts is formulated as a methodological tool. This classification divides the intellectual thought into two main categories: modernity in Focus and modernity marginal. Each category is further divided, and the thought of each intellectual representing each main current is reviewed, discussed and analyzed in detail. Building on this classification, the analysis of the thought of Sadik Jalal al-Azm represents the extreme secular current, whereas the thought of Mohammad Arkoun represents the moderate secular current. While the ideas of Sayyid Qutb represents the Salafi current, the thought of Mohammad Abid al-Jabiri represents the reconciliatory current. The analysis clearly demonstrates the divers macro-perspectives of these intellectuals particularly in their interpretations of the causes of backwardness, and the agenda proposed for solutions and social change in the Arab World. In addition, this study shows a noticeable gap between the macro-perspectives of the intellectuals and the findings of some empirical micro-studies. This study demonstrates the inadequacy of relying on one single approach and proposes the integration of both macro and micro perspectives. Therefore, this study suggests integration between the macro and the micro perspectives in interdisciplinary studies about the social reality of the Arab World. [Author Abstract]

2.)   **Bakhtiari, B.**

Religion and politics: The Middle East and Latin America.

Ph.D. dissertation, University of Virginia.

1984.

The interrelationship between religion and politics has always been a major question in the study of politics. Before the emergence of the idea of "secular" society and its subsequent spread around the globe, the ultimate goals of religion and politics were generally indistinguishable. Questions of dividing and delimiting two spheres of life, secular and sacred, were not at issue. However, the "resurgence of Islam" in the Moslem world in general and the Middle East in particular, and the emergence of "liberation theology" in Latin America show graphically the need for broadening and deepening the study of this interrelationship by exploring the experiences of different societies. This study attempts for the first time to compare and contrast the ideas of a selected number of major Moslem and Christian thinkers from the Middle East and Latin America. The leading thinkers included are examples of both "traditionalist" and "revolutionary" schools of thought within both the Islamic and the Christian traditions. From the former tradition, the work of Aytollah Khomeini from Iran, and of Sayyid Qutb from Egypt, have been examined as representative of the traditionalists school of thought, and those of Ali Shari'ati, also from Iran, as representative of the revolutionary school of thought. From the latter tradition, the works of St. Augustine and of Juan Donoso Cortes have been examined as representative of the traditionalist school of thought, and those of Gustavo Gutierrez as representative of the revolutionary school of thought. The major findings of this dissertation include both similarities and differences between the Islamic and Christian responses to the challenges of modern society. Both the traditionalists in Catholicism and the classicists in Islam oppose secularization, especially its ideological components of liberalism and socialism. They emphasize the divine origins of government and authority. However, they differ on theological questions. The revolutionaries are similar in that they de-emphasize the religious, metaphysical aspect of Islam and Christianity, and that they use such concepts as class analysis and dialectical materialism. [Author Abstract]

3.)   **Barnes, L. A.**
Sayyid Qutb: "Pious hero of Islam" or terrorist theoretician?*
M.A. thesis, The University of Kansas. 2006.

Sayyid Qutb is best known for his writings, membership within Egypt's Muslim Brotherhood, and martyrdom at the hands of Nasser. This thesis examines Qutb's life, three of his major Islamic writings (Social Justice in Islam, In the Shade of the Qur'an and Milestones), his influence on modern Islamic fundamentalism, and his connection to some of the world's most notorious terrorists. As the paper reveals, sixty-years after his death, Qutb continues to play a powerful role in a radical movement to conduct global jihad and implement a total Islamic state. The world is presently engaged in a war against radical Islamism and terrorist tactics. Understanding Qutb's ideology and his influence is one more baby step towards understanding and defeating an

enemy that seeks to harm people worldwide.
*"Pious hero of Islam" taken from Richard P. Mitchell, The Society of Muslim Brothers, New York: Oxford UP, 1993, 208. [Author Abstract]

4.) **Bouzid, A. T.**
Man, society, and knowledge in the Islamist discourse of Sayyid Qutb.
Ph.D. dissertation, Virginia Tech University. 1998.

Sayyid Qutb's conceptions of man and society inform and are themselves informed by his theory of human and divine knowledge. Our aim in this dissertation is, first, to highlight the intricate relationships between Qutb's ontology and his epistemology, and, second, to point to the active context of Qutb's discourse: how did his theory of man, society, and knowledge relate to his language of political dissent and his strategy for change and revolution? Qutb remains an enduring influence on young Muslims and has left a deep mark on the discourse of politically activist Islamism. An underlying concern that runs through our analysis will be to address the question: why is Qutb still relevant? The answer we provide highlights the inseparability between Qutb's conception of human nature, his paradigm for the just and ideal society, his theories on mundane and revealed epistemology, and his strategy for social and political reform. We shall argue that the Qutbian discourse endures because Qutb offers his co-religionists a powerfully integrated conception of the "Islamic solution" that achieves a unique blending between the values of "authenticity" and those of "modernity." Qutb's writings articulate an unapologetic "life-conception" of Islam that insisted on standing on par with other "life-conceptions"; Muslims could take pride in knowing that Islam exhorted development, but with an eye towards maintaining a "balance" between the "material" and the "spiritual," unlike communism and capitalism, which neglected "spirituality" in favor of "animal materialism"; the "Islamic conception" outlined by Qutb provided the reader with a conceptual framework within which a sophisticated critique of colonialism could be carried out. Moreover, Qutb also provided the modern Islamist with a vocabulary that gives voice to the economic and social concerns of an emerging lower middle class aspiring to fulfill its mundane dreams in modern, mid-20th century Egypt. The language Qutb used in his works was not the language of the elite intellectuals, whether Westernized modernists or traditional 'ulema. Qutb consciously articulated his thoughts in a language easily accessible to a readership literate enough to read his works, but not necessarily trained to actively penetrate the arcane corpus of the 'ulema. Upon reading Qutb and contrasting his language with that of his predecessors, it becomes clear that Qutb, more than any other thinker in the Egypt of his days, articulated a conception of Islam that consciously attempted to lay the foundations for an Islamic epistemology on the basis of a putatively Islamic ontology, denied the authority of "foreign life conceptions," claimed for Islam universal validity, asserted the active character of the "truly Muslim," decried the economic injustices which the masses were enduring, and rejected the traditional conception of the state as intrinsically benevolent. In short, his was a powerful call to merge the values of authenticity--unapologetic anti-imperialism, anti-elitism, and the insistence on the centrality of Islam--with the values of modernity--the impulse for asserting a comprehensive world-view, the pretension to universal validity, and the positive valuation of action and change in the context of welfare liberalism beholden to the will of the people. [Author Abstract]

5.)   **Bozek, J. D.**
Sayyid Qutb: An historical and contextual analysis of jihadist theory.
M.S.C.J. thesis, Grand Valley State University. 2008.

The purpose of this research is to provide a comprehensive analysis of a salient jihadist philosopher by the name of Sayyid Qutb. Qutb is arguably among the most influential ideologues of modern-day Islamic militancy; yet, there is very little research examining his works. Through in-depth analysis of the historical, social, and political contexts surrounding Qutb and Islamic militancy, this research will examine selected works of Qutb to determine the frequency of his use of militant language and how his usage of militant language relates to his overall ideology; place Qutb's writings into historical, social, and political contexts while at the same time examining if, and how, they are influencing militants today; and, identify the importance of understanding the beliefs conveyed by Qutb for the purpose of informing counterterrorism policy. [Author Abstract]

6.)   **Calvert, J. C. M.**
Discourse, community and power: Sayyid Qutb and the Islamic movement in Egypt.
Ph.D. dissertation, McGill University (Canada). 1993.

Through an examination of the life and writings of the Egyptian Islamist Sayyid Qutb (1906-1966), this dissertation seeks to determine the conceptual bases of the Islamic movement in twentieth-century Egypt. It is argued that the central factor in the rise of islamically-oriented opposition to the elite order has been the gradual emergence in Egypt of the distinctively modern form of the nation-state. Specifically, the processes of Egyptian State formation are seen as responsible not only for the creation of conditions conducive to oppositional Islamism, but for engendering notions of national community and historical transformation which, through the processes of discursive transmutation, have provided the core of political sentiment undergirding this particular form of dissent. [Author Abstract]

7.)   **Edens, M. H.**

An evangelical Christian response to concepts of humanity found in selected Islamic writings.

Ph.D. dissertation, New Orleans Baptist Theological Seminary. 1993.

The purpose of this research is to analyze evangelical Christian apologetic implications of the Islamic concept of humanity, as expressed in the formative documents of Islam and selected contemporary Muslim writings. Three types of primary data are employed in this study. Passages from classical Islamic documents, El Qur'an and el Hadith (The Sayings of the Prophet), are one type of primary data. The writings of Naguib Mahfouz, Gamal Abd al Nasser, and Sayyid Qutb are a second type of primary source. The Christian Bible in its original languages is a third type of primary data. Historical research methodology is employed in this study. The primary data for the first and second subproblems are contained in Arabic documents. The Arabic passages were located, translated, and critically analyzed. Deviation from the classical position were examined and interpreted as to implications for apologetics. Three hypotheses were investigated in the study. All three were supported by the research. First, the study demonstrated that the classical Islamic documents, el Qur'an and el Hadith, contain statements on human nature and purpose. Humanity was created as one family by God. All persons are responsible to obey the Creator. The corporate nature of humanity is expressed in relationships within the family and society. The pattern of Islamic society expands the relational principles found in the family. Second, research supports the hypothesis that the writings of Naguib Mahfouz, Gamal Abd al Nasser, and Sayyid Qutb express changes in the classical Islamic concept of humanity and that these changes can be discovered. Mahfouz, Abd al Nasser, and Qutb each ignored content of classical Islamic humanity according to their interests and concerns. Each emphasized one of the three aspects of humanity under study to the detriment of the remaining two aspects. Finally, the study demonstrated that Islamic views of humanity have implications for evangelical Christian apologetics. Corollaries between evangelical Christian views of humanity were discovered. Principles for effective communication with Muslims were drawn from the writings of Christian workers among Muslims. Apologetic implications of the selected views of Islamic humanity then were framed. Beginning from the human ideals and needs expressed in Muslim writings, an explanation of the person and work of Jesus of Nazareth, the Christ, was proposed. [Author Abstract]

8.) **Elfenbein, C. H. I.**
Differentiating Islam: Colonialism, Sayyid Qutb, and religious transformation in modern Egypt.
Ph.D. dissertation, University of California, Santa Barbara. 2008.

Sayyid Qutb is often rendered as a backward looking, anti-modern figure. This portrayal suggests a serious misunderstanding of his theory of history and, by extension, the relationship between the foundational sources of Islam and the life of the Muslim community. In broader terms, it reflects an understanding of modernity grounded in secularization orthodoxies, or the expectation that modernization entails a conclusive differentiation of religion from other spheres of life. However, to account for the dynamic presence of religion in public life something other than an aberration, it is necessary to re-think this characterization of differentiation. This dissertation applies a reconceptualized understanding of differentiation as an ongoing process to offer a reading of Sayyid Qutb as a quintessentially modern voice in debates about the nature of religion. So doing, it also presents a fruitful theoretical framework to explore religion and public life in modernity more generally. Grounded in a critique of differentiation, Qutb's work is part of modern debates about the question of human welfare, particularly as they unfolded in eighteenth and nineteenth century Great Britain with the emergence of utilitarian thought. This dissertation shows that despite great temporal and geographical distance, Qutb's systematic Islamist vision is in conversation with utilitarian traditions regarding differentiation in the foundations, logics, and ends of collective life. This dissertation draws on three sources to establish this connection: the work of John Locke, David Hume, Adam Smith, Jeremy Bentham, and James Mill; the annual reports and other materials filed by Lord Cromer, chief British consular official in Egypt from 1883-1906; and the work of Sayyid Qutb, most especially Ma'alim fi al-tariq (Milestones) and Hadha al-din (This Religion). This dissertation also draws on secondary literature from philosophy, history, anthropology, sociology, and of course religious studies. Certainly, Qutb's participation unfolds as part of ongoing Islamic traditions of welfare. But it comes in conditions of possibility radically transformed by British colonial administration. As a participant in debates over differentiation that are characteristic--if not constitutive--of modernity, his historically novel "undifferentiated" vision of Islam suggests the commingling of Islamic traditions with modern forms of knowledge and authority. [Author Abstract]

9.)   **Elgindy, A.**

Translation and the construction of the religious other: A sociological approach to English translations of Islamic political discourse.

Ph.D. dissertation, University of Salford (United Kingdom). 2013.

Translations of texts associated with the phenomenon known as `political Islam´ into English remain largely unexplored. The main objective of the current thesis is to develop a sociological model for the study of translations of Islamic political discourse, based on the work of Pierre Bourdieu. The basic assumptions of Bourdieu's sociological theory are adapted to formulate a methodology for the study of translations of Hassan al-Banna's Towards the Light, and Sayyid Qutb's Social Justice in Islam into English. The thesis discusses in detail Bourdieu's sociology of cultural production, its intellectual foundations, theoretical tools, and methodological relevance to both translation in general, and translation of Islamic discourse in particular. The research hypothesizes a field of activity which could be called `the field of translating political Islam´ in the Anglo-American culture. The dynamics of this field and its structure are premised on the notion of struggle over specific forms of capital between producers and co-producers of translation in this context. Bourdieu´s key concepts of field, habitus, capital, and doxa, are used to both describe and interpret the activity in this field. They are also used to provide a sociological insight into the production and consumption of translation, as well as the translatorial agency within this field. [Author Abstract]

10.)   **Euben, R. L.**
Islamic fundamentalism and the limits of modern rationalism.
Ph.D. dissertation, Princeton University. 1995.

In this dissertation, I offer an interpretation of Islamic fundamentalist political thought in an attempt to provide a window into fundamentalists' own understandings of the movement's meaning and purpose and contribute to explanations of the increasing power of fundamentalist ideas in the contemporary world. My analysis of Islamic fundamentalist political thought entails a critique of the Western modes of political analysis that have been used to interpret fundamentalist thought and action. My aim is to use this critique to illuminate the limits of Western rationalist theoretical categories, and concomitantly to demonstrate both the possibility and the necessity of an internalist approach to understanding Islamic fundamentalism, and of critical and evaluative criteria that do not depend upon access to standards of truth outside of language and history. In analyzing Islamic fundamentalist political theory, however, I also seek to illuminate some of the relationships between contemporary Western and Islamic political thought. In particular, I argue that one of the most influential theorists of Sunni Islamic fundamentalist thought, Sayyid Qutb, is engaged in a critique of rationalism that we in "the West" not only recognize, but in which we frequently participate. Such a comparative analysis simultaneously works against the tendency in the West to regard Islamic fundamentalist thought as pathological or culturally idiosyncratic and illuminates Western ambivalences regarding modernity and rationalism. It also serves as an occasion to elaborate the methodology of what I call comparative political theory, that is, the attempt to ask questions about the nature and value of common involvements in a variety of cultural and political contexts. By introducing non-Western perspectives into debates about common dilemmas of living-together, comparative political theory insures that "political theory" is about human and not merely Western dilemmas. [Author Abstract]

11.)   **Frisk, W. H.**

The Vanguards of Islamism: Origins, Histories, and Ideologies of the Society of Muslim Brothers in Egypt.

M.A. thesis, University of California, Santa Barbara. 2013.

The pivotal role Islamism will play in the post-Arab Spring global dynamic drives this thesis. It analyses the various origins and ideologies of the most seminal Islamist movement, the Egyptian Muslim Brotherhood. As Egypt serves as the socio-political fulcrum of the Middle East North Africa region, so too stands the Muslim Brotherhood as the logical genesis for a discussion about the larger phenomenon of Islamism. My thesis argues that the Brotherhood specifically, and Islamism generally, offers far more flexibility in ideology than the West frequently concedes. Its development proves non-linear, complex and frequently interrupted by bifurcation; the ideologies it produced and still produces are therefore polymorphic, ranging from moderate and conciliatory to belligerent and radical. Which, if any, Islamism prevails in the Middle East will depend on the abilities of the various movements' leaders to offer beneficial alternatives to the decades of tyranny the masses rejected in the Arab Spring. I argue that by returning to the ideology of the Brotherhood's founding father, Hassan al-Banna, a moderate, conciliatory, and above all flexible interpretation of Islamism may be found. This requires a reconsideration of the radicalism that has spiraled out of the ranks of the Brotherhood, specifically acknowledging Sayyid Qutb's writings as aberrations of al Banna's message, rather than as natural evolutions. I conclude that Islamism and radical Islamism must be separated in academic and political discourse, treated as related but separate phenomena, in order to push the quotidial dialogue in a mutually generative direction. To do this, I first trace the historical trajectory of the Brotherhood, highlighting incidences of flexibility and cooperative methods of the movement to insure its survival through the tumultuous post-Colonial era. The second section highlights the Brotherhood's oscillations between radical and moderate ideological positions. My analysis demonstrates that the Muslim Brotherhood has a long history of pragmatic response to changing political situations. The West too often views the Muslim Brotherhood through the "Clash of Civilization" narrative -- in which the Muslim Brotherhood is one continuous, fixed entity in opposition to the West -- rather than acknowledging the bifurcated and malleable identity of the organization. [Author Abstract]

12.)   **Gelineau, J.**
Threat and Political Opportunity and the Development of the Egyptian Muslim Brotherhood.
M.A. thesis, University of Kansas. 2011.

In order to better understand the Muslim Brotherhood's role in contemporary Egyptian politics, this paper studies how the Brotherhood's development has been shaped by interaction with the strong secular state and the changing political environment. By examining how social movements develop in authoritarian states, this paper demonstrates the effects of threat and political opportunity environments on the Muslim Brotherhood. The use of escalating state repression caused some elements of the Muslim Brotherhood to splinter off and form violent extremist organizations, while enabling political participation through increased institutional access and participation in competitive elections caused the mainstream Muslim

Brotherhood to moderate and work toward democratic reform within the system. [Author Abstract]

13.) **Hassan, F. M.**

Ending oppression and establishing justice: Examples from Islamic history of select Muslims and Islamist groups justifying the use of armed force.

Ph.D. dissertation, Florida State University. 2006.

This dissertation examines the justification for using armed force throughout Islam's history. Special emphasis will be made to the following three terms, harb, jihad, and qital. These three words translate into war, struggle, and fight respectively. Not only are these terms the catalyst for the expansion of Islam in its first century, 632 to 732, but they have also contributed to many ideologies. The origins for such ideas begin in the seventh century and Islam's most prominent religious figure, Mohammed. It is only fitting that the first chapter of this endeavor starts with his life and the reasons why he went to war with others. As his life showed, he never declared a "jihad" on others, a term that is used constantly in the media. It is important to remember that according to Muslims, Mohammed never did anything out of his own opinion; it was all done with the endorsement of God. The Qur'an and Ahadith will also be examined, as they are the major sources for justifying and conducting war. After the death of Mohammed in 632 however, armed force began to take on a different meaning. This work covers Mohammed, the Kharijites, the Assassins, Ibn Taymiyya, Sayyid Qutb, al-Jihad, and al-Qaeda, with emphasis placed on Mohammed and Qutb as key figures, and their respective justifications for using or writing about resorting to armed force as a means to an end. During this dissertation, comparisons will be made between all of the before-mentioned Muslims and their respective reasons for fighting or writing about the use of armed force. It is the main thesis of this work that violence committed in the name of God by Muslims throughout Islam's history is based upon the need to end oppression and establish justice. This dissertation differs itself from other written works by solely examining the life and works of individual Muslims and Islamist groups and their justification for resorting to armed force. Though this topic has gained momentum since the events of 9/11, it is the intention of this work to show that using armed force is not new, but a political instrument used to establish Shari'ah or Islamic law. The term "political" is used because for most Muslims, including all those mentioned in this dissertation, believe that Islam is not just a personal belief system, like most in the West believe, but an ideology that is to be used for all times and for all facets of life. [Author Abstract]

14.) **Hawwari, A. A. S.**
Challenging the incompatibility paradigm: A democratic audit of Jordan, 1990-2010.
Ph.D. dissertation, Westminster College (United Kingdom). 2012.

This thesis assesses the state of democracy in Jordan over a period of twenty years (1990-2010), and revisits the claims of incompatibility between democracy and both Islam and Islamism. It subjects the claims to theoretical and empirical tests. This is possible through a case study of Jordan. The state was established by Britain, and is ruled by a dynasty, which highlights its lineage to the Prophet of Islam, Muhammad. Jordan also allowed the Muslim Brothers to take part in the process characterised by King Hussein in 1989 as the `resumption of our democratic life.´ Incompatibility is taken to mean that Islamic teachings prohibit adopting democracy as a system of government, as Qutb and Mawdudi have argued; and that democracy cannot take root in a Muslim society because the state and church (mosque) are inseparable, as argued by Lewis and others. The thesis outlines the procedure Muslim jurists use to declare an act or a notion to be allowed (halal) or forbidden (haram). It also engages with various democratic theories including the argument that democracy is `an essentially contested concept.´ The thesis establishes that, theoretically, Islam is not incompatible with democracy, whether as claimed by Qutb and Mawdudi, or Lewis and Huntington. Moreover, the thesis posits that if the democratic audit establishes that Jordan is a democracy, the compatibility of democracy and Islam is validated empirically. The audit revealed that Jordan was not a democracy. The roles of Islam and Islamism in hindering the development of democracy in Jordan were examined. The evidence indicated that they did not. Therefore, other reasons were examined, such as rentierism, Arab-Israel conflict, and Rustow's modernisation theory. The latter offers the most plausible explanation, as Jordan has not satisfied Rustow's four antecedents to democracy. The Islamist groups have not yet managed to be in power through democratic means. It remains debatable whether they will adhere to democracy after it brings them to power. The case of Jordan provides counter-evidence that the Islamists can hold the belief that Islam provides a superior form of government, but can simultaneously play by democratic rules. One could even argue that in Jordan there was a case of a democratic paradox in reverse. [Author Abstract]

15.) **Horowitz, J.**
An examination of how American business must eliminate perceived bias towards Muslims and Arab Americans.
M.A. thesis, State University of New York Empire State College. 2010.

Following September 11, 2001, America realized that we were no longer protected by our borders and that our enemies managed to extort our vulnerabilities. This event forever changed commercial aviation and transportation as a whole, as well as directly impacted how many of us view Muslims or those who we perceive to be Muslims. I examined and concluded through a synthesis of ideas that American Business must eliminate perceived bias towards Muslims and Arab Americans. The American-Arab Anti-Discrimination Committee Research Institute, and polls conducted by the University of Washington, Yale University, and Genesis Research demonstrated that a perceived bias exists towards Muslims and Arab Americans post 911. From September 11, 2001 through December 11, 2002, the EEOC received 705 Title VII charges (Title VII of the Civil Rights Act of 1964 strictly prohibits workplace discrimination and harassment specifically based on national origin and religion). Furthermore, this bias proved costly to American business because Title VII Harassment Claims were awarded; as of August 2003, ninety-two people who alleged harassment received more than 1.425 million dollars in monetary compensation. In order to understand why Islamic Fundamentalists consider Americans their enemies, we must first recognize how an individual evolves into a fundamentalist. After reviewing a large body of literature, I am convinced that Osama bin Laden received his fundamentalist ideology through a history of Wahhabi education originating and sustained through the Debandi movement and facilitated by the teachings of Sayyid

Qutb. These conclusions are demonstrated through numerous books and articles written by Paul Berman, Jonathon Randal, and Robert Siegel to list a few. In addition, I focused on the Islamic Fundamentalist ideology, specifically, I am convinced that Osama bin Laden as well as other Islamic Fundamentalists view that violence, martyrdom, and the Jihad are all justified in the name of Allah. This conclusion was a result from numerous books, articles, and research papers from such authors as Gilles Kepel, Mahmood Mandani, and the Library of Congress Congressional Research Service. Moreover, that Islamic Fundamentalists believe that their form of Islam cannot co-exist with any other religion, including other sects of Islam. To prove that Islamic fundamentalism is not accepted and practiced by most, I provided the traditional or mainstream Muslim view on violence, martyrdom, and the Jihad. I concluded from a synthesis of ideas that mainstream Islam not only condemns martyrdom and the killing of innocent people, but defines the Jihad as an inner struggle to attain God's three thousand qualities, contrary to the fundamentalist interpretation as a holy war. I presented evidence that the basic tenets of traditional Islam are peace, and that history demonstrated tolerance towards non-believers since the Middle Ages. I concluded this through numerous books, articles, and websites from Vartan Gregorian, Abdullah Momin, David Dakake, and the Council on American Islamic Relations. [Author Abstract]

16.) **Hosein, J.**

A Cross Examination of Sayyid Qutb and Muhammad Ibn Abd Al-Wahhab.

M.A. thesis, University of Alberta (Canada). 2012.

This thesis is a cross examination of the life and writings of Sayyid Qutb and Muhammad Ibn Abd al-Wahhab. The main thesis argues that both Qutb and Ibn Abd al-Wahhab largely interpreted Islamic doctrines in light of their own relevant political issues. Through the process of legitimating their political struggles through Islamic texts they distorted the image of Islam to suit their own purposes. The thesis tries to assert the relationship between the religious interpretation of these two Islamic scholars and compare them based on the critical analysis of relevant scholarship. The conclusion of this thesis, in accordance with this view, is that Islam does not advocate compulsion in religion and that militant religious extremists like Qutb and Ibn Abd al-Wahhab have used the teachings of Islam to further their own political agendas, rather than apply a profoundly insightful interpretation of the sacred texts. The final goal of this thesis is to advocate an increased awareness and renewed dialogue between the spiritual aspects of Islam versus the political or legal aspects of Islam. [Author Abstract]

17.) **Isaacson, T. J.**

Miracles and militancy: The evental origins of religious revolution.

M.A. thesis, University of Denver. 2013.

Utilizing the theoretical framework of philosopher Alain Badiou, this paper will examine the force and movement of religiously fueled, revolutionary politics. Badiou's definition of event is read through the theological concept of miracle, put forward by jurist Carl Schmitt in order to elucidate the inauguration of new order. The theological concept of miracle radicalizes Alain Badiou's definition of event by manner of divine authorization. While Schmitt uses miracle to explicate sovereign preservation of the State, and Badiou's interest lies in its erosion, reading both thinkers through miracle, and through each other, conceptualizes the theo-political militant, authorized by event to interrupt orders and enact new law. The first chapter begins with an analysis of Badiou's event, politics and militant fidelity, harnessing his framework while critiquing what is not counted in his recent work Rebirth of History. The second chapter will discuss Carl Schmitt's sovereign and its link to the theological concept of miracle. The chapter demonstrates miracle's conceptual similarity to event, excepting that within its interruption is the investiture of divine authorization. The final chapter will examine the case study of Sayyid Qutb and his text Milestones to exemplify that Badiou's framework bolstered by the theological concept of miracle accounts for the diverse disruptions of national, economic, and cultural orders along with the prescription for new possibilities. [Author Abstract]

18.)   **Jackson, R. A.**

A Nietzschean approach to key Islamic paradigms.

Ph.D. dissertation, University of Kent at Canterbury (United Kingdom). 2003.

Islam and the West, it will be argued, are not as incompatible in a civilisational or ideological context as history might suggest. Compatibility can be better appreciated by examining what are regarded by Muslims as key paradigms that make up Islamic identity: that of the Qur'an, Muhammad, Medina as the first 'Islamic state', and the four 'rightly-guarded' (rashidun) caliphs. To be Muslim is to accept certain archetypes as central to belief. This is not what is in contention. However, what is a matter of contention is how one approaches these paradigms, particularly amongst such renowned Islamic revivalist scholars as

Mawlana Mawdudi, Muhammad Iqbal, Sayyid Qutb and Jamal al-Din Afghani. This thesis argues that the approach has been dominated by what is termed the 'Transhistorical': mythologizing the paradigms to the extent that they have become 'idols' which its adherents are unwilling to question or even, if necessary, to shatter. The Muslim philosopher Mawlana Mawdudi will be represented as symbolising this Transhistorical approach. However, another approach can be usefully adopted, that of the Historical, that perceives the paradigms within the context of time and place, thus allowing for flexibility of constant renewal and reassessment. The German philosopher Friedrich Nietzsche can be helpfully employed in examining the Historical approach. Whilst Nietzsche rarely spoke specifically about Islam, his admiration for it as a religion is in sharp contrast to his criticism of Christianity. Whilst Nietzsche was addressing an audience of a different culture and age, this thesis aims to show that his philosophy can make an important contribution to the dialectical understanding between Islam and the West. [Author Abstract]

19.)   **Kozak, A. M.**

Reconceptualization of democracy from an Islamic subaltern.

Ph.D. dissertation, University of Minnesota. 2013.

This dissertation challenges a dominant trait in contemporary western thought that understands Islamist politics as holistic and antithetical to modernity and democracy; that presents Islamism as an expression of traditionalism in the modern world. I challenge this dominant western perception by asking the question: how have the ideologues and the founders of the most well known Islamic movements of the Muslim world approached democracy, a modern political system, and related it to an Islamic state? Addressing the dynamic relationship between Islamic political thought and socio-political context, with this dissertation, I offer a critique of this literature, which positions the Islamic world as an archaic civilization in an inevitable clash with the West, the representative of modernity. By analyzing the original works of two well-known ideologues of Islamic movements from Indo-Pakistan and Egypt, I depict the ways in which Islamic political thought intervenes in cardinal conversations about democracy. There are four main goals of this dissertation. First, I recover the story of modernity in political thought from the two different parts of the Muslim world. Second, I reveal the voices of Muslim intellectuals in the meaning making and indigenization of a western-originated idea, democracy, into Islam. Third, I challenge a dominant discourse that puts Islam and the West as civilizations in a clash. Fourth, I point out the necessity to engage non-western political theory to enhance our intellectual endeavors and rid the literature of its Eurocentric biases. To achieve these goals, a comparative historical analysis method was utilized based on two cases: Sayyid Qutb and

Mawdudi's conceptualization of democracy. In analyzing the data, I employed analytical narrative method in tracing patterns of causal factors as well as in making causal inferences through the comparison between and within these cases. Throughout the study, I pursued a dual analytical agenda, which included examining how each ideologue defined democracy, how these ideologues related democracy and Islam to each other, and how the local and international events and institutions uniquely shaped their ideas regarding democracy. Findings indicate that, both Mawdudi and Qutb opened up the idea of democracy to a new set of critiques and methods of adaptation. For Qutb and Mawdudi, being an imported product of colonial and capitalist world, democracy was not to be implemented to the Muslim world directly. It had to be supplemented with indigenous forms of explanation and interpretation to make sense within existing political realities.

Criticizing the slavish imitation of western democracies, they recommended a political system based on local representation. They believed that governments would achieve greater legitimacy if the political structure and language of politics were in line with the culture and beliefs of the people. They emphasized the match between the cultural meanings, values, and beliefs of Islam and democracy. They raised questions regarding certain dogmatic assumptions implicit in the concept, which they identified as part of the secularist/capitalist/colonialist project. Mawdudi and Qutb's works reveals that the western democratic model cannot and should not be replicated in the Muslim world because, at the economic level, it presumes capitalism, and at the social level, it presumes individualism and secularism. Their solution was to create their vernacular political language and terminology to work with the idea of democracy which they named as theodemocracy by Mawdudi and

Islamic state by Qutb and strictly refrained from using western terminologies like republican, democratic, or socialist to define their systems. [Author Abstract]

20.) **LaRossa, C.**

The development of Islamic political thought in relation to the West during the mid-twentieth century.

Ph.D. dissertation, University of St. Andrews (United Kingdom). 2011.

This research is about the development of Islamic political thought in relation to the West during the mid-twentieth century. It utilizes the ideas and writings of the Islamic thinkers Sayyid Qutb of Egypt, Ali Shariati of Iran, and Jalal Al-e Ahmad of Iran to illustrate this development. These figures reacted severely to Westernization (argued to constitute colonialism, materialism, and secularism) as they saw it. This research will argue that their reaction was due to the fatally corrosive effects each figure believed this was having upon Islamic civil society and the Islamic moral economy, both in their respective home homelands and throughout the greater global Ummah. Their perspective is unique because they were critiquing the West based upon their experiences while in the West, and using Western intellectual ideas to do so. This was done, this research contends, in reaction to aspects of Edward Said's Orientalism discourse. Qutb, Shariati, and Al-e Ahmad's reaction to the West, this research also argues, displays aspects of Friedrich Nietzsche's thought, namely that when an entity (in this case, Islam) encounters the West, God is lost in that encounter. Additionally, this research argues that Qutb, Shariati, and Al-e Ahmad sought to counter the loss of God in Islamic civil society and halt the influence of Westernization as they saw it via the political realm through the use of the Quran as law and government, thereby permanently restoring God to Islamic civil society and salvaging the Islamic moral economy. [Author Abstract]

21.)   **Leary, J. D.**

Beyond Al-Qa'ida: The theology, transformation and global growth of Salafi radicalism since 1979.

M.A. thesis, American University. 2002.

Contemporary Salafi Radicalism finds its religious roots primarily in the theology of Muhammad Abdul-Wahhab and Sayyid Qutb, while its social roots stem from the cultural, social, political and economic crisis faced by Muslims in the latter half of the 20th Century. These circumstances, along with the Afghan Jihad, led to a transformation of Salafi Radicalism in the 1980's, in which the Saudi and Egyptian expressions of Salafi Radicalism merged. This resulted in an emergence of a radicalized Salafi assemblage that drew in many existing Salafi radical groups in the Muslim world. The end result was a network of semi-independent extremist groups, each capable and willing to commit violent acts against civilians. In order to counter this threat the United States, along with it's allies, must work to defeat the Salafi Radical movement through a combination of military pressure, cultural undermining of radicalism and economic development. [Author Abstract]

22.)   Moussalli, A. S.

Contemporary Islamic political thought: Sayyid Qutb.

Ph.D. dissertation, University of Maryland College Park. 1985.

Sayyid Qutb (1906-66) is one of the most outstanding writers on Islamic fundamentalism, for his teachings about the institution of an Islamic state and the application of the divine law have taken root and become prevalent in the Muslim world. Because he has provided Islamic fundamentalism with its most important intellectual bases and because of his execution by the Egyptian government, he is now the symbol of the advocacy of fundamentalist thought. My treatment, analytical rather than historical focuses on the intellectual and political foundations and principles of fundamentalism. Because the dissertation deals with the adequacy and logic of fundamentalist principals and ideas, the method used is analytical, not historical. Chapter One deals with biographical and bibliographical matters. It analyzes the style of Qutb's writings; his use of primary and secondary sources; and, the characteristics, division, and consistency of his writings. Chapter Two focuses on the principles and ideas that Qutb relies on to explain, discuss, and advance his theories. It analyzes his "universal Islamic concept," itself consisting of seven main principles given by Qutb: namely, <u>tawhīd</u> or oneness of God, divinity, fixedness, comprehensiveness, balance, positiveness, and realism. Comparisons between him and other Muslim thinkers are drawn in order to place him in the field of contemporary Islamic thought. He believes, for instance, in the inadequacy of human thought to understand the universe. Qutb's conclusions are modern in content, but cast in the form of religious fundamentalism. Qutb's exposition of the concept of <u>tawhīd</u> goes from metaphysics and philosophy back to political and economic principles. These principles and their application – discussed in chapter 3 -- become a must for the creation of a good state. The good state is characterized by obedience to the divine law, social justice, and a revolution that brings about and maintains the good state. It should, for instance, provide free education and social guarantees and uphold morality. Morality, as manifested primarily in the upbringing of the family, is the cornerstone of a good state, and the function of the leader of this state is to protect morality as taught in the Holy Qurān. The only true moral principles are to be found in the Holy Qurān because, according to Qutb, human reason is incapable of attaining certitude. For history shows Qutb that people have worshipped many gods and accepted many principles that are even contrary to common sense. The logical conclusion that Qutb arrives at is that human thought should not be the foundation for morality and truth. This conclusion leads him to attach those who believe that human though is the instrument of attaining the truth. He argues that our present miseries are the result of too much dependence on our reason and our neglect of the true foundation of everything, i.e., God. Finally, in the Conclusion as well as in the main body I discuss the significance and importance of his teachings on the intellectual as well as on the political level and provide a critical summary of his thought. [Author Abstract]

23.)   **Mubarak, H.**

Intersections: Modernity, gender, and Qur'anic exegesis.

Ph.D. dissertation, Georgetown University. 2014.

Modernity imparted a new theoretical significance to the issue of gender reform in the Muslim world. This dissertation examines the impact of modernity on the hermeneutical approaches and interpretations of three modern exegetes on significant gender issues in the Qur'an. It compares the tafsir works of Muhammad 'Abduh, Sayyid Qutb, and Muhammad al-Tahir ibn 'Ashur with those of pre-modern exegetes concerning three Qur'anic verses: 2:228, 4:3, and 4:34. These verses, among others, gained significance in modern exegetes' quest to articulate Islam's position on gender, a debate that was tied to the larger ideological question on whether or not Islam was fit for modern times. By situating the exegeses of 'Abduh, Qutb, and Ibn 'Ashur within their broader historical and intellectual contexts, this dissertation demonstrates how their tafsir on gender reflects their engagement with the broader contemporaneous debates on gender and Islam in late-nineteenth- and mid-twentieth century Egypt and Tunisia. The interpretations of all three modern exegetes evince a heightened gender-consciousness that is absent from the interpretations of pre-modern exegetes on the same verses. This underscores the particularity of an exegetical gender-consciousness to the modern period. The tension between continuity and change in modern Islamic intellectual thought demonstrates that interpretive differences between modern and pre-modern exegetes are not black and white. While 'Abduh, Qutb, and Ibn 'Ashur reach significantly new conclusions on certain verses, they also echo many of the pre-modern interpretations on gender. As such, the exegetical tradition on gender reflects a variety of interpretations that defies existing generalizations of this tradition as consistently patriarchal. While the works of all three exegetes reflect full engagement with modernity, their approaches are grounded in very different methodologies, traditions, and orientations. This dissertation argues that 'Abduh and Rida 's Tafsir al-Manar and Qutb's Fi Zilal al-Qur'an both signal a departure from the classical methodologies of the pre-modern exegetical tradition, whereas Ibn 'Ash ur's al-Tahrir wal-Tanw ir revives the methodologies of the pre-modern, philological exegetical tradition. As such, Ibn 'Ashur represents the classical Sunni practice of renewal based on pre-existing scholarly norms. [Author Abstract]

24.)   **Munro, M. A.**

Religion and revolution in Egypt.

M.A. thesis, McGill University (Canada).

1997.

The purpose of this thesis is to analyse the relationship between religion and revolution within the context of Egyptian Islamic culture. The discussion will begin with an investigation into the evolution of revolution as a concept, from its original scientific meaning within the writings of Copernicus to its current political meaning as a radical social break with the past. It will be argued that the revolutionary ideal of escaping fate and rationally constructing the future is the driving force behind the Modern era. Faith in the capacity of humanity for self-redemption could only arise after the scientific discoveries of the Renaissance began to disrupt the static metaphysical universe of the past. The concept of social development then arose in the Enlightenment as a quest for the liberation of reason so as to construct a new society free of myth and mystery. The discussion will then attempt to demonstrate that the culture of Egypt underwent a parallel philosophical development during the nineteenth and twentieth centuries due to the importation of modern technology. In order to prove this, the military reforms of Muhammad `Ali will be compared to Hobbe's concept of the Leviathan, the journalism of Muhammad `Abduh will be placed within the traditional Islamic debate concerning the ethical relationship between reason and revelation; the cult of nationalism will be contrasted with sûfî mysticism; the social project of the Nasser regime will be interpreted in light of Rousseau's conception of the liberal social contract; and the thesis will conclude with a discussion of the thought of Sayyid Qutb in terms of the failure of Modernity to fulfil the promise of the Enlightenment. [Author Abstract]

25.) **Musallam, A. A.**

The formative stages of Sayyid Qutb's intellectual career and his emergence as an Islamic Da'iyah, 1906-1952.

Ph.D. dissertation, University of Michigan. 1983.

This is an inquiry into the genesis of the career and thought of Sayyid Qutb, poet, educator, journalist, literary critic and a leading intellectual of the contemporary Islamic movement who was executed in Egypt in 1966 on charges of leading a conspiracy to overthrow the Nasser regime. This study places the greatest emphasis on an analysis of Qutb's intellectual transformation prior to the July 1952 "Free Officers" military revolution and his emergence as one of the leading ideologues of the Society of Muslim Brothers. However, an overview of Qutb's 1952-1966 career is also presented in the concluding chapter. Findings indicate that Qutb was a product of a society which had been going through major political and cultural dislocations at a time when Egypt's transition from a traditional to a modern society was taking place. In the 1920's and 1930's Qutb was very much influenced by secular forces, especially the Wafd Party, the modernist Abbas Mahmud al-Aqqad and the Diwan school of literature's rebellion against neo-classicalism. Qutb, however, became increasingly alienated from the status quo because of rampant Westernization and the failure of the ruling establishment to achieve independence of the Nile Valley and to solve society's pressing problems. World War II and the economic, political and social dislocations it caused further alienated one-time adherents of liberal nationalist ideals like Qutb. The impact of World War II on Qutb is very much reflected in his writing; it was during this period, that many drastic changes began to take place in Qutb's outlook and he became increasingly more interested in the study of the Qur'an. Despite the fact that in the period between 1939 and 1947 Qutb was stressing the purely artistic or literary goal of his Qur'anic studies, the long-lasting spiritual effect of his deep study of the Qur'an is clear. His unhappiness in Cairo which was very much evident in his prose and poetry in the 1930's and 1940's, the death of his mother, his shattered love affair, his poor health and his alienation from the status quo and from Western civilization prompted him to turn increasingly toward the Qur'an for his personal needs and for answers to his society's ills. [Author Abstract]

26.)   **Mussad, H. W.**
Muslim debate on the adoption of the Shari'a and its implications for the Church.
Ph.D. dissertation, Fuller Theological Seminary. 1996.

This study is a theological analysis of the arguments of the Muslim fundamentalist Sayyid Qutb (1906-1966) and that of the Muslim modernist Muhammad Sa'id al-Ashmawi on adoption of the Sari'a. The debate on the Sari'a has its implications for the Church of Jesus Christ. This study is an attempt to understand the Muslim debate on adopting the Sari'a. The fundamentalists disagree with the modernist Muslims on the issue of how to apply the Sari'a and what the Sari'a is. Each of the two schools, the fundamentalist and the Modernist, has a different interpretation of the Quran. Each tries to find legitimacy from either the Quran or the Sunnah. A brief account is given on how each school interprets a particular verse from the Quran. A biblical response on the matter of the Sari'a is also included. To understand the background of the debate between the two schools, this study includes a brief account of the history of the fundamentalist movement in Egypt. Although the Muslim fundamentalist movement is taking place in many other parts of the Muslim world, Egypt has been the center of the intellectual debate between the modernist and fundamentalist Muslims. Although the Muslim fundamentalists are not the figures of political authority in Egypt, yet the Muslim fundamentalist movement in Egypt is considered the mother of all of the other fundamentalist movements in the Muslim world. In a hostile environment, the Church of Jesus Christ is required to follow certain biblical commands. This study attempts to clarify these biblical principles. [Author Abstract]

27.) **Mussad, H. W.**

Theology of the Muslim fundamentalist Sayyid Qutb.

M.A. thesis, Fuller Theological Seminary. 1989.

This study is a theological analysis of Fi Zilal al-Qur'an, a 30-volume commentary on the Quran in Arabic by Sayyid Qutb (1906-1966), the major ideologue of the largest contemporary fundamentalist group in the Arab World, the Muslim Brethern. Comparisons are made between his theology and Christian theology to determine bridges and obstacles to Christian interpretation. Comparisons are also made between his fundamentalist views and these of other Muslims. The greater stress he puts on the all-inclusiveness of Islam makes conversion more difficult. His consigning of Christians, and even Muslims not ruled by Islamic law(shari'a) to ignorance (jahiliyya), limits the reservoir of common belief and practice for Christian interpretation. Likewise his rejection of the second coming of Christ, though it is affirmed by many Muslims, eliminates one of the major areas of common faith. [Author Abstract]

28.) **Oh, I. Y. I.**

Human rights in contemporary Islamic thought: Toward a cross-cultural discourse ethic.

Ph.D. dissertation, University of Virginia. 2004.

Human Rights in Contemporary Islamic Thought is an experiment in comparative religious ethics. I analyze the writings of Sayyid Qutb, Abul A'la Maududi, and Abdolkarim Soroush to show how a range of Islamic thought contributes to the cross-cultural dialogue necessary for the progression of universal human rights. The chapters of the dissertation, arranged thematically, offer a comparative understanding of the issues at stake. The first two chapters provide histories of the last century, focusing upon the Universal Declaration of Human Rights (1948) and colonialism in Muslim countries. The inclusive process of drafting the Declaration sets an auspicious precedent for the incorporation of Islamic voices in human rights. Documented participation in creating the UDHR by representatives of countries such as Egypt, Pakistan, Lebanon, and Saudi Arabia helps to ensure the acceptance of human rights in Muslim countries. The effectiveness of cross-cultural dialogue becomes especially apparent in the writings of Qutb and Maududi, who despite their criticisms of the UN and wariness of cultural imperialism, readily accept the validity of rights language. Following these histories are three chapters that focus on the views of Qutb, Maududi, and Soroush concerning "democracy," "toleration," and "freedom of conscience." These discussions reveal not only their beliefs about these aspects of human rights, but also their relevant epistemologies and attitudes towards the West. The final substantive chapter examines the possibility of dialogue between Islamic thinkers and human rights theorists, including Michael

Ignatieff, Jack Donnelly, and Henry Shue. Non-foundational human rights models, espoused by Ignatieff, or models based upon Western paradigms, as recommended by Donnelly, are likely to alienate Islamic thinkers in cross-cultural discourses. Shue's observation of correlative duties as complementary to rights, however, presents a potentially useful framework for engaging Islamic scholars in the human rights debate. Fears of the threat to human rights posed by religious difference need to be balanced by the ways in which religions, including Islam, have contributed to the acceptance and implementation of human rights. By acknowledging the complexity of Islamic thought and finding common ground, a universal human rights ethic becomes possible. [Author Abstract]

29.)   **Rahman, S.**

The concept of takfir (accusing of disbelief) among some contemporary Islamic movements with special reference to Egypt. Ph.D. dissertation, University of Birmingham (United Kingdom). 1994.

The widespread practice of *takfr*, accusing an opponent of being *kfir* (unbeliever), among some contemporary Islamic movements today makes it necessary to consider the meaning of *kufr* (unbelief) in early Islam. In the Qur'n, the concepts of *kufr, nifq* (hypocrisy) and *irtidd* (apostasy) are related; they, therefore need to be discussed. This thesis concludes that the judgement of whether an individual is *kfir* is God's not man's. A study of the Sunnah of the Prophet Muammad shows that he was always very reluctant to apply the term *kufr* to individuals. When he did, he was very lenient in their treatment. *Kufr* continues to be a sensitive subject among more recent theologians in their consideration of *'aqdah* (belief), and the relationship between faith and action. The concept of *takfr* which has been adopted by the radical Islamic movements since 650 C.E. is not related to the question of belief, but rather to the political problems and the legitimacy of rulers. From the first civil war (the Battles of the Camel, 36H./657C.E., and Siffin 37H./657C.E.), the concept of *takfr* has been used for political purposes. Branches of the Kharijites were especially inclined to condemn all opponents as unbelievers, making it legitimate to seek them out and kill them. For many Shi'ites, unbelief in the Imamate amounts to *kufr*. The more radical trends, like the Kaysniyyah, accepted the consequence that they could be killed. But, the Immiyyah (Twelvers) took the view that believers should mix with unbelievers, and their punishment was to be left to God. Sayyid Qutb, one of the key thinkers of the Muslim Brotherhood, like the Kharijites and some branches of the Shi'ites, introduced the concept of *takfr*, which was opposed by the Supreme Guide of the organisation (asan al-Hudayb). [Author Abstract]

30.) **Roald, A. S.**
Tarbiya: Education and politics in Islamic movements in Jordan and Malaysia.
Fil.Dr. dissertation, Lunds University (Sweden). 1994.

The present study deals with theories in the field of Islamic education and these theories actual application in some Islamic movements in Jordan and Malaysia. Islamists regard Islam as a complete system (nizam shamil) covering all aspects of human life. Thus, in their view, Islamic education deals not only with matters of formal education but with all fields of society such as politics, economics, and social relations. Islamic social scientists have elaborated ideas in the field of Islamic education both at the level of formal and non-formal education, but a firm theory has yet to be moulded. Through literary analysis and fieldwork in Malaysia and Jordan, I could contrast the theoretical foundation of the Islamic social scientists with the actual practices of the Islamic movements. Results of the research showed that to a great extent theory and practice were not in concordance. The discrepancy between theory and practice was also found within particular movements, as for instance in the case of the Muslim Brothers' organization who theoretically emphasizes intellectual development in an academic sense of the word, whereas the actual practice in its Islamic schools proved to be more in line with the didactics in Jordan in general with memorizing and recipient learning. The study discusses relations between leaders and members of Islamic movements. It also conceptualizes Islamic movements. To Bryan Wilson's scheme of sect responses, I added four categories of response: tawhidic, ideological, rational, and educational. My overall impression was that Islamic movements are heterogeneous and a product of environments, linked to economical, political and psychological conditions. Even though many of the movements intellectuals are influenced by ideas promoted by Islamist classics, such as Hasan al-Banna', Sayyid Qutb and Abu al-'Ala Mawdudi, the movement intellectuals tended to adapt these ideas to their own local environment. [Author Abstract]

31.) **Salihu, F.**
Assemblages of radicalism: The online recruitment practices of Islamist terrorists.
Ph.D. dissertation, Arizona State University. 2014.

This dissertation explores the various online radicalization and recruitment practices of groups like al-Qaeda and Hezbollah, as well as Salafi Jihadists in general. I will also outline the inadequacies of the federal government's engagement with terrorist / Islamist ideologies and explore the ways in which early 20th century foundational Islamist theorists like Hasan al-Banna, Sayyid Qutb, and Abul ala Mawdudi have affected contemporary extremist Islamist groups, while exploring this myth of the ideal caliphate which persists in the ideology of contemporary extremist Islamist groups. In a larger sense, I am arguing that exploitation of the internet (particularly social networking platforms) in the radicalization of new communities of followers is much more dangerous than cyberterrorism (as in attacks on cyber networks within the government and the private sector), which is what is most often considered to be the primary threat that terrorists pose with their presence on the internet. Online radicalization should, I argue, be given more consideration when forming public policy because of the immediate danger that it poses, especially given the rise of microterrorism. Similarly, through the case studies that I am examining, I am bringing the humanities into the discussion of extremist (religious) rhetorics, an area of discourse that those scholars have largely ignored. [Author Abstract]

32.)   **Sayilgan, M. S.**
Constructing an Islamic ethics of non-violence: The case of Bediuzzaman Said Nursi.
M.A. thesis, University of Alberta (Canada). 2012.

This thesis examines the late Muslim theologian Bediuzzaman Said Nursi's ethics of nonviolence. It argues that the non-violent ethics of Bediüzzaman Said Nursi based on the Qur'an might aid in finding solutions to the global problem of religion and violence, particularly as it is experienced in the Muslim World. The research seeks to accomplish three objectives. First, this study aims to contribute to the increasing number of works in the area of Islamic ethics which are still minimal compared to the literature dealing with Islamic law. The second scope of this project therefore focuses on the examination of the ethics of non-violence as presented in Said Nursi's writings. Though Nursi never applied violence and constantly encouraged his followers to avoid it, he is still not known as an Islamic figure who promoted non-violence. The third objective is to demonstrate the ambiguity within the Qur'an when it comes to defining a clear stance on violence. This will be evident through the juxtaposition of Said Nursi with Sayyid Qutb. [Author Abstract]

33.)   **Shah Bin Jani, M.**
Sayyid Qutb's view of jihad; an analytical study of his major works.
Ph.D. dissertation, University of Birmingham (United Kingdom). 1998.

It has been claimed that the current phenomenon of radicalism in the Muslim world was a result of the fundamentalist movement's struggle to establish Islam as a social order. Usually, such radicalism was linked with the interpretation of jihd of influential thinkers of the Islamic movements, like Hasan al-Bann, Abu al-A͑l al-Mawdd, Sayyid Qutb and others. The aim of this study is to have a critical analysis of Sayyid Qutb's view of jihd, which is one of the major components of his religio-political discourse. It is also aimed at providing an objective response to the claim that Sayyid Qutb's view of jihd was responsible for the violence involving some militant Islamic groups in the Muslim world in the name of

Islam. Sayyid Qutb's view of jihd is a synthesis of the classical and the modernist interpretation of jihd. Influenced by the bi-compartmentalization of the world into two: Dr al-Islm and Dr al-Harb, Sayyid Qutb saw the present world, including the Muslim world, were under the domination of jhiliyyah, i.e. an un-Islamic state of affairs similar to that which was prevalent among the Arabs during the pre-Islamic history. The purpose of his jihd was to liberate the world, including the Muslim world, from the bondage of jhiliyyah, and to reconstruct an Islamic society in which Islam is established as a system of life. This jihd requires the formation of an Islamic group whose members are founded by a group of dedicated vanguards (al-al^cat al-Islmiyyah). Sayyid Qutb's jihd was a call for a total revolution against a political establishment which is oblivious to Islam and hostile to exponents of the Islamic mission. [Author Abstract]

34.) **Shaikh, E. M.**

War and peace: Towards an understanding of the theology of jihad.

M.A. thesis, University of North Texas. 2004.

The growing number of terrorist attacks waged by Islamic fundamentalists has led to an increasing desire to understand the nature of jihad. These attacks have led to a renewed sense of urgency to find answers to such questions as why these attacks occur, and who they are waged against. Towards this end I turn to examine the political philosophy of four Muslim theologians. Specifically I look at the political philosophy of Sayyid Qutb, Shah Walai Allah Dihlawai, Ibn Rushd (Averroes), and Muhammad Sa'id al-Ashmawy. I find that the notion of jihad is very inconclusive. Furthermore, the question of jihad revolves largely around the question of whether or not individuals can be reasoned with, and secondly whether religion should be compelled upon individuals. [Author Abstract]

35.)   **Steiner, J. G.**

The psychology of terrorism: A case study of Osama bin Laden.

M.A.L.S. thesis, Georgetown University.

2012.

Sociologists and psychiatrists often contend that culture, religion, social and economic factors are precursors to extremist Islamic ideology. According to Robert Robins and Jerrold Post in their groundbreaking book, Political Paranoia: The Psychopolitics of Hatred, paranoia is the hallmark of radical thinking. Post and Robins argue political paranoia is responsible for every social disaster in history and is among the root causes for the decline of the West. This thesis will test Robins' and Post's hypothesis by conducting a case study of Osama bin Laden. Specifically, I explore significant events in bin Laden's life that drove him to cross the line from paranoia into psychopathy exhibited by his propensity to eliminate perceived enemies and his remarkable ability to manipulate others. This includes convincing a worldwide network of Muslims that the West seeks to destroy Islam. Using the work of Robins and Post to establish the foundational concept of political paranoia, along with Frances Fukuyama's theory of the end of history, and Dr. Robert Hare's notion of the psychopath, this thesis explores how these phenomena impacted bin Laden's reasoning. To accomplish this, I examine bin Laden's formative years to assess how family, religion and events in Egypt and Afghanistan shaped his thinking. The philosophy of Sayyid Qutb, ideologue of the Muslim Brotherhood, is highlighted to demonstrate that al Qaeda's ideology is simply a repackaging of Qutb's works to justify martyrdom as an ethical form of jihad and piety. Notably, Qutb considered America to be morally bankrupt and secular government to be an affront to Islam. This notion was adopted by bin Laden to justify his hatred of the Saudi government and the West. In conclusion, I assert bin Laden sought to turn Islam against the West to establish a new Islamic regime with himself at front and center. After the September 11 attacks, a decade of war, and an economy that cannot sustain a bloated security apparatus, the West has been forced by terrorists like bin Laden to become paranoid for good reason. [Author Abstract]

36.) **Suarez-Murias, A.**
"Jihad is the way and death for the sake of Allah is our highest aspiration": A narrative analysis of Sayyid Qutb's "Milestones."
M.A. thesis, Wake Forest University. 2013.

The volatile dynamic between radical Islamists and Western society is well established, often revealing itself through violent acts of terrorism. This ongoing conflict has prompted a spike of critical interest in the communication between extremists and the outsiders they perceive as enemies, generating a fuller understanding of extremist ideology critical to counter-terrorism efforts. While this intergroup communication has remained a focus among scholars, the intragroup communication within these radical groups is also of significant importance and has remained widely unexamined. This intragroup discourse allows group members to develop shared perceptions of identity and the nature of their conflict with the outside world; it is this process of sensemaking that justifies and enables the often-violent action of extremist groups. This project takes an important step toward an understanding of radical Islamism with a comprehensive analysis of a text widely cited and regarded as instrumental in developing the ideology of today's radical Islam: Sayyid Qutb's Milestones. A close rhetorical critique of the text will illuminate how Qutb's work creates meaning through a narrative that defines the worldview of his adherents. The aim of this analysis is to inform a counter-narrative strategy to challenge and prevent the continued spread of radical ideology. [Author Abstract]

37.)   **Syahnan, M.**

A study of Sayyid Qutb's Qur'an exegesis in earlier and later editions of his "Fi Zilal al-Qur'an" with specific reference to selected themes.

M.A. thesis, McGill University (Canada). 1997.

This thesis is an attempt to analyze Sayyid Qutb's approach to Qur'an exegesis in his Fi Zilal al-Qur'an. It compares the earlier with the later revised editions of the exegesis as it studies change in his thought and Weltanschauung. Qutb believed that the sacred text was a book of guidance and inspiration with immediate relevance to contemporary issues and challenges, giving direction to practical affairs as though it had been revealed specifically for today's problems. It is suggested that social, political, economic, and psychological factors contributed to his interpretation and revision. The thesis explores the degree of the revision made as well as its significance, with special reference to the case of zakat (alms) and riba (usury)-related verses in particular. Although the fundamental stance is basically consistent, i.e. that Islam is a distinct, divinely-ordained system for all aspects of life, it shows that Qutb tended to draw sharp distinctions between those who strove for the establishment of God's law in the world, and those who opposed them. Thus, in his exegetical endeavour, he became inevitably influenced by his socio-political background, and his exegesis was different from other contemporary ones, because it expressed the views of an activist advocate of social, political and religious reform, even though his thought was at times vague and idealistic. [Author Abstract]

38.) **Winkel, E. A.**
The ontological status of politics in Islam and the epistemology of Islamic revival.
Ph.D. dissertation, University of South Carolina. 1988.

The study of Islamic revival poses special problems to the modern analyst of social change both because Islamic revivalists often make truth claims about Islam that are irreconcilable with modernism and because certain concepts in Islamic politics--such as "non-separation of church and state"--meet with tremendous resistance from modern political philosophy. The most sophisticated level of criticism for studying "alien" cultures--post-modernism--because it cannot allow certain Islamic assumptions, fails to bring a full appreciation of Islamic revival. The solution to this dilemma is in my thesis that mystic attempts in Islam to remove the veil correspond to the reduction of epistemologically distorting interests in post-modern criticism. We can co-opt the tools of the post-modern critic, while remaining in the Weltanschauung of Islamic revivalists, and thus accomplish two things. First, we achieve a full understanding and appreciation of Islamic revival, and second we can turn the tables and arrive at a logical, systematic, and persuasive critique of post-modernism itself. This work examines classical Islamic revivalists who are sufis or who are influenced by sufism and sacred wisdom (`irfan), namely Ibn al-`Arabi, Abu Hamid Ghazali, Ibn Khaldun, and Shah Wali-Ullah. It then analyzes modern revivalists (who often borrow from these classical revivalists) such as `Ali `Abd ar-Raziq, Sayyid Qutb, Maulana Maududi, and Ayatallah Khumayni. The contrast between liberal ideology, which is central to some Western thought and some Islamic fundamentalist thought, and `irfan is brought out as a foil to the analysis of these revivalists. [Author Abstract]

39.)   **Yunus, M. R.**

Modern approaches to the study of i'jaz al-Qur'an.

Ph.D. dissertation, University of Michigan. 1994.

The theme of i jaz, the inimitability of the Qur'an, is one of the important dogmas in Islam. Many books have been written concerning this issue from the second/eight century to modern times. Traditional authors concede that the i jaz of the Qur'an is its rhetorical excellence (balaghah), because it it this aspect that presents and explains the nazm (composition) of the Qur'an, and hence, its tahaddi/ (challenge). In modern times, i jaz remains a major issue for Muslim authors. But unlike their predecessors, modern authors do not emphasize solely the theme of balaghah. Instead, they consider the unique style of the Qur'an as only complementary to more important aspects of the Holy Book, which are its contents and message in general. This study is concerned principally with an examination in detail of the modern approaches to the issue of i jaz partly by comparison with classical writings on this subject and partly by elucidation of new ideas. It finds that some of the modern views of the i jaz are only a continuation of traditional ones, though some of them use new terms, and some authors give more arguments for their theories. It also finds that some modern approaches have an important relation to the way one interprets the Qur'an, such as, for example, are observable in views of Sayyid Qutb and Bint al-Shati'. Critical study of the works of these authors indicates that the modern view, to some extent, had tended to shift the study of the Qur'an from a verse-to-verse method in traditional discussion of i jaz to different methods, including among them a tendency towards a holistic approach. [Author Abstract]

Locating Dissertations and Theses

A. Purchase

Many of the dissertations and theses listed in this bibliography are available for purchase through UMI Dissertation Express:

> http://disexpress.umi.com/dxweb

By Fax:

> 800-864-0019

By Mail:

> 789 E. Eisenhower Parkway, P.O. Box 1346, Ann Arbor, Michigan 48106-1346
>
> 800-521-3042

B. Interlibrary Loan

Dissertations and theses may also be requested through Interlibrary Loan via your local public, college or university library.

Printed in Great Britain
by Amazon.co.uk, Ltd.,
Marston Gate.